OF YOU
AND OTHER PATHS

OF YOU
AND OTHER PATHS

Third Collection of Poetry

CONCETTA BATTAGLIA

Arts In Media

Library of Congress Catalog Card No: 96-96886
ISBN No. 0-9654032-0-3

Published by
Arts in Media
P.O. Box 499
Lindenhurst, New York 11757-0499
Cover Design: Joseph Battaglia
Printing: Bilmar Printing & Graphics – Lindenhurst, New York 11757

CONTENTS - *First Line Title Poems*

CONTENTS - *First Line Title Poems* - Continued

Dedicated
to the gifts
we each possess

I am
In a deadline
With myself.
I must meet
The setting sun.

I am a creature of the night
Placing fancies into flight.
As stars gaze down on me
I soar
Into
Their open luminous core.

Moon?
I look for you.
I see your light
Glinting
On the leaves.
I see the bark
Of the tree
Radiant
With sight.
Moon?
I go to you
With open arms
And I embrace
Your winning warmth.
Moon?

Is it change of season
That causes me to slumber
With troubled eye
And weary thunder
Of promises
Not kept
And beginnings shattered
That force mute cries
Unanswered?

The moon is dim
In the frame of space -
A portrait of mystery
Covers its face -
Knowing the darkness
And showing its light
It penetrates dreams
With welcoming sight.

I spent the night
In troubled space
Floating thoughts
Of vacuity -
Impatient
For
The bird's first call
Summoning
Life
Into me.

From the emptied womb
Erupts the virgin brink
Of heady skies
And molten volcanoes.
The ether permeates the cells
And calls them to another place.

Thunder rumbling
In the night
Leaves a burst
Of broken dreams
Waiting
To be struck
By lightning

Their eyes
Locked together
And the key
Remained
Bound
In each other's
Soul

Sweet pain
Quiet turbulency
Lost am I
In reverie
And the moon still finds its way
Through the clouds

Sweet scent
Of summer night
Where amber moon
Was last night white
The white butterfly
Flutters
By green space -
I wait.

The sweetness
Of the summer earth
Draws blossoms
From the nighttime girth -
As petals drop
From starry paths
I breathe the mist
Of rainy baths

Why
Do crickets sound
A thin staccato song
In the dying night?
Is it because
Our destinies
Are brought together
By the chirping rhythm
Of that dawning light?

I lowered the shade
And closed down the day
Where shadow of oak
Looms clear in display
I entered the night
And drew up the stars
While the moon pulled me
Into
A familiar par.

The moon tucks its face
Behind that dark cloud
As I
Hide from you.

But oh, the soft night!
Where light dreams
Become realities
And tender thoughts
Are love songs
We will meet, my love
And dance in the mist
Until stark life
Makes its recall

The moon is so bright
It stretches
Into the room -
Before heady dawn strikes
The moon
Will have its full

Blue light
Surrounds
The white scepter
Of moon
Constant
In its muted space -
A day sky
Vanishes
Without a trace.

The cricket chirps
To a spaced-out
Moon-filled night.
The stars strike
The silent song
And the gasps of breath
Become shorter.

I kissed your last tear
And treasured it
To my lips.
Your lifeblood became
Absorbed into mine.
That one droplet
Flooded my presence
And washed away
The pain
Of the moment.

These two lovers
Having
Found themselves
Washed
By the sea's caress
Could not
Be united
In life
But
Now
There is
The distant eternity
Where
Seas touch stars
And
There is
One.

I await the moon
And
The moon
Answers
My call.
I shine my face
Upon the moon
As round lights
Path my span -
And the moon
Comforts me
While crickets
Mark their exit.

Blank eyes
Light dimmed
Soft cries
Heart skimmed
Love shorn
Too late
Forlorn
Locked strait

Inbound
As a fossil -
Searching
For a find
To
An outbound existence
Where petrification
Takes place
Daily

The invading forces
Enter the lonely cavity
In mock attack
Only to find
An emptied love.
They leave the camp
In disquietude.

A chill has entered
The marrow of the bone
Where Arctic air penetrates
The empty cells
And one is left
In vacuous solitude
As a lifeless leaf
Resting
On the pine

A wide-winged crow
Gliding
About in the sun
Black body against white
Defies our plight
As it moves knowingly
From brown bark
To emptied branch.
And
Homebound with fever
I watch
That ominous sight
As the years stretch tight
Into
Snowbound light.

Waves lap onto
A waiting shore.
Drawn by the force
Of sand-filled store
They breathe
Eternal ether stone
And calm soft presence
Left alone.

The moon tides the handles
Of man
As it hovers
In soft gleaming span -
A persistent clock
That holds calm power
And charts all waiting
To final hour.

The moon
Is on the half-rise.
The stars
Are there to wish on.
The cricket
Chirps its last song
In October.
The autumn
Sends its cool breath
Through
Wood-filled earth.
And
I
Sense
Ashes
In the ether.

It is suddenly light
Here in the night
With the moon in cloud
And squirrel nest waiting -
The branches are clear
Spread out and pointing
To all anchors
That moor the earth.

Before the leaves fall
Into total recall
I will guide your light
In the wintry day
Where dawn
Will reign forever

What is "forever"?
Is it a day, a year, a century?
Is it from the beginning
To the end?
Is it that which arrives
At a time in destiny
When stars collide?
Is it when atoms spray kaleidoscopes
And white light permeates all?
Or is it this moment
This wholeness of now -
This thought which magnifies
Very existence of being?
Here is forever -
Time held in tow.

The day is closing in
On a winter
That will begin
Its journey
Of a full moon sky
Where new moments
Test the dye.

I pulled the moon down
From its neighborly sky
And held it close
To my searching dream.
I took the crystal ball
And found its light -
Then rose with the moon
To the star-borne night.

Drops of buried icicle
Touch the tiniest leaf
Of time
Melting into earth -
Memories of yesterday
Evacuating graciously
Into a pendulum
Of tomorrow's chill.

The moon and I
Await each other.
We whisper soft words
In moving ether
And glow
At our sweet responses.
We are companions
In the night.

This long, starry winter night
Where sparkles space
In timeless sight
There between the branches hung
As white bright sheet
Of jeweled tongue -
I breathe soft air
Of bondage lair
And wonder
In sweet captive stare.

Winter tree
Stark in sight
Thrown askew
Through
Dayborn night
As dusk
Arrests
The waiting calm
And dawn
Contains
The threadbare arm

The moon awaits
In sun-bathed clouds
Pacing through
The evening shrouds
Sentry
In the full-fledged night
Viewing
All who give it sight -
Exulting
In enraptured charm
I pass into its wafted arm.
O darkness,
Light my inner eyes
For dawn comes swift
In your demise.

The crows hover over rooftops
Black on white shingle
In early spring
When birds bring promise
And mourning doves
Call to the lonely air

The moon shone in a halo
That spread into the night
A saint on its mission
Spreading the light.
Who could fear that face
With benign smile of grace?
Not I.

I freed those moments
From the past
And placed them in
A molten cast -
Those moments
When my heart soared fast.
I bounced
An image into space
And caught its flight
In star-tracked trace.

The moon leaves a silhouette
Of tree branches
Spread into the night.
It is my mirror
In space.

In winterspring when leaves still blow
Heavily on the oak tree show
I look upon them with sad heart
Knowing they and I will part.
My eyes will watch with knowing gaze
As grey brown turns to budding graze
And when the rain soaks lovely bark
So will time lay traced in dark.

The last remnant
Of winter
Clings to the tree -
It aches for release
But knows gentle winds
Tease it into endurance.
New buds look upon
This aged stranger
With curiosity
Befitting new life -
They cannot imagine
Why in winterspring
When all cycles are memory
One would be lingering -
Seeking, languishing -
In spring.

The leaves turned
Silver-green today.
They were heavy
With gray yesterday.
I could swear
I kept watch
From day to day -
But
They formed spring
While I looked away

The moon is my companion
Through the night
As straddling forth
We walk the sight
Of starry-eyed trees
And sleepy-eyed seas.
We are as one
The moon and I -
Gazing at dreams
And scanning the sky.

A rapt watcher
Awaits the discerning entry
And looks longingly
At its presence
With smiles
Lit
By the moon.
Spirits are free

I kiss the setting sun
As it lowers itself
Over painted spires.
Bidding it love
I await each star
That accompanies
The new entry
Of captured light.